FAR DISTRICT

POEMS

ACKNOWLEDGMENTS

Grateful acknowledgment is made to the following publications, in which some of these poems originally appeared: *Calloloo Journal, Caribbean Review of Books, Pathways: Journal of New Writing, Poetry International, Southern Humanities Review, The Wolf Magazine*, and *Town*. "Anthropology" appeared in the anthology *So Much Things to Say*.

CONTENTS

for May
1930-2008

THE TURNING ROAD

Schooldays, I travelled the narrow
bridge separating St Thomas
and Portland; warm pubescent blood

beat in my ears along the road
snaking through cane flags that cowered
their yearly death in the reaping

fire. Behind, the bush's lore:
mongoose, ghosts and rolling-calves;
up ahead, the sea's greater myth:

sea-salted ports drunk off sunlight.
As I crossed over, a sibyl sang
at the hemline a welcome.

I never stopped at that axis,
but one morning I slowed; in the middle
of the path, a carcass: a dog's, a mule's, a hog's,

its rotten smell circled by john crows.
Not roadkill, the skull crushed
into stones, attended by acolyte-flies,

but a sacrifice that simply dropped dead
in the night. I felt responsible
to seal its rite by the stagnant canal

dividing the lane from the asphalt.
The sea ruled half of me; the other,
a pitched nothingness. So I turned back.

ANTHROPOLOGY

The houses are shut, the neighbours gone
to the burning field at the mangrove's edge,
where the heatstruck anthropologist writes
his prophecy in a wrenched tense:
"Their Gods… they've drowned."
All day I choke on the pages' knotted vines:
the totems will be covered, the Revivalists'
prayer poles, the rain woman's dance,
her rattle sticks beating the earth, until
the clothesline quivers like a Spanish
fly, pressed to a concrete block
by a boy, aiming his blunt needle.

The workers will return at dark, at the beetle's horn,
to the shack alley, to the rasps of Sankeys
on the dead man's moth-meshed veranda;
they will gather for nine nights to the prophet's
rum-riddled call, with coco pods, mint bush,
cerasse, Bay Rum, Bible leaves and Phensic –
they will gnash teeth and groan epiphanies
with swaying bottle lamps over the fowl's blood
spilled on the ash, and on a body, with the dead's
tongue, warning all before morning. Frenetic,
without proper exegesis, I cut stone-cold
through the bush-lane home.

But the sugar-headed children will wander
the field at night, lost to the scavenging
green, eating the ripe flux of the land,
and then emptying their guts in the river
no longer worshipped, now a machine,
like the factory's tractor passing, loaded
with burnt canes, their foreheads white
with marl dust. Their eyes burn, gazing

at the half-yam moon – their tribe's
biography, a possession they cannot read.

They clatter away, children and tractors,
threading the coiled sleep that will not loosen
into the meagre flash beyond suffering –
the light opening a book towards a simplicity
hard to achieve, though they are simple saints.
In the final dusk they head for the hill
holding up the sky, the shutterless, dozing shacks –
the hill they will rise to before work and play,
the hill that will rise before tomorrow's dead.

SOME NEGATIVES

My long-ago body, face down in the grass.
Think about it in brushstrokes of yellow.

A rat-gnawed moon, Mr. Bell's spirit
unbuttoned the night, and slipped out.

The poison cherry tree was in bloom:
under its red, orange and green, boys played marble.

Shield your eyes; below this line's
my father's death: memories don't ever go past Bryan's Bay.

A bike gutted through the rut, then sputtered
dead, we found the engine heap, oil mixing blood.

In the middle of the school path was a beehive,
and between that and that, nothing but bushes.

On my last night, rolling calves dragged their chains
around the house, bellowing my name until morning.

HOUSE ON THE HILL

In the morning, I am in Trakl's
drying poppies, his baroque
style leaning towards violence.

Books line the windowsill,
jagging the frost-panels,
variable without directions.

Somewhere is
such a kingdom. Not this
ice-locked landscape;

the Keybank's red neon
glares throughout the night,
the devil's key in my sleep

and my sleeplessness.
Morning surrounds
my grandmother's hill,

finds her yellow
house empty, the sea-rusted
grille locked, the yard fly-stunned.

The mud gutter gapes,
a frightening parenthesis
as if hardest hit

by her departure; the pickaxe's split
tongue thrusts in the ackee tree,
sap gluing shut its iron lisps,

mute; only the ants bustle
in their new commerce, crossing
the acre with funerary burdens.

Many summers' shade
I have spent under that tree,
busy with the plebeian ants,

waiting for my late mother,
grandmother brooding
on the veranda. Proconsul

of the sea, I didn't hear
the house's arthritic timbre
unfurled into the yard,

the paint shedding, the kitchen
beads dropping tears
on the red-polished floor;

I didn't hear the leaf's
winding curl down to the soil,
settling solidly there,

an upturned caterpillar
resembling a dusk-coloured urn,
earth, that rusty rainwater drum.

My ears, tuned to the blue
above and below, had already captured
Trakl's music, his taut

string of poppies, shrill-echoed,
not even her death disturbed –
only now, reading him, butterfly

furies startle from self-cursed
pages, that hill, with her chiton voice,
and beat their wings in my throat.

REQUIEM FOR AUNT MAY

I

A calm sign in the trees of May: she's dead,
not like this dirge staining the air, her name
recited in the camphor-house where the chalk
figurine, that haberdashery sphinx reclines,
riddled by the TV. There no one faces the calendar,
river-stone talks go under the bridge of condolences,
and land on the old sofa's shoulder. I, her water-child,
keep watch over her laminated Saviour, nailed
into the wall, flipping a coin whose head promises
Daedalus. Someone pries open an album, the cocoon
postcards wail on the line, pronouncing, *Aunt May* –

baker, builder of the yellow stone house, your children
hatched wings while your face was bent in the oven.
The mixing bowls, the wooden spoons, the plastic
bride & groom, knew before the phone alarmed
the night your passing. So you passed, in a floral dress,
a shawl softly tied to your head, the house spring-cleaned.

II

Enters Daedalus, father, dressed in white, hands
in pockets, strolling through prayers and smoke
of the mourning wake. I listen: his limbs
are pure starch! On the veranda, eyeing
the gong-tormented sea, seaweeds streak
his beard, salt rimmed his apologies. I hesitate
at the labyrinth of father and son, red hurt
throbbing my ears from my fall on the poppy grounds,
fog swallowing all that was carried over
years of saying nothing. Silence, this flame

held back before erupting, as an oven after heat
has been sucked from it. I begin in silence
my life, then and there, as a ghost.

CATCH FIRE

Old Shiduri came out evening,
her bare feet edging the ash yard,
avoiding the paved road since
she poisoned her son and husband –

so the story went – who owned
the slaughterhouse, *A & Son*.
Parents warned: "Never go near that
old-higue, coolie-witch, else skin will catch

fire and hell and powder house to pay."
So when I see her she is invisible,
but one fine silk day, a tamarind-breeze
rustled her silver hair in a pale shawl,

her web-mouth trembled to itself
as I neared, a wasp danced in my head –
not a soul in sight – so I hailed her,
then hit the pavement home, craze-wings

in rage, excitement solid. It dissolved
at the zinc gate, where mother waited
with a shaved stick, her mouth a vexed-snag
hole. After the first whip-sting, the myth

went out of the day. No mercy, welt-fledge,
I yelped down the whole district, who begged her,
"Bird, ease up the boy." But she locked them out,
closed me in the small room and I squealed,

"I will break the door, wrench the lock, and let in the dead."

But she did not understand and night fell
over the lit field and on her hard face –
a breathing dark, her eyes, two steady white slits.

THE MOTHER PORTRAIT

Nyame, my mother, you are sick.
I am afraid, as if I were in darkness
and slit-white eyes are mocking me.
The healer woman says you've been marked,
that your enemy put a coolie duppy
on you, so mornings when the basil
rise in the nose, the duppy is outside.
Nyame, why you? You never trouble people,
you don't hang with rum-head district
women on the plaza, cutting eyes, lapping
skirts on people's business whole day.
They call you things, I hear them –
Lady-a-the-Night, Ninny, Bird –
the dishtowel names hang on fences
to quail in the sun for all to see.
What wrong you caused, what damage?
Is it us, your two precious
that you boast of, our father
who ran away to the streets of England,
we who wear shoes out of
the once-in-a-blue moon parcel
to school and eat out of crockery,
and must not romp with village pickney?
Nyame, did I fertilize their envy
and push their hands to obeah?
To watch you turn fool, madwoman
running across yards, chased by a white-hair,
shrilled-voice coolie duppy.
Nyame, I see you sick and hurting
and I can't help you, I afraid
to look in your eyes or touch you,
my own mother! It kills to watch
your mouth corner froth and dry
with the sickness, the strong smell

of healer's potions in your skin,
oil in your creases, in your ears and neck,
and your wrists tied to the bed;
vomit on your bosom, blood in your torn hair,
fury in your grunts and screams.
Nyame! My mother, you are sick!
But you are not dead, not yet,
though that horror is in your eyes,
and I piss myself like a boy
who's lost and hungry in the night
swamp where morning will not light.
Oh God, Nyame, I am too weak
and I am watching you dying
while my sister sleeps on the floor,
her dreams troubled by the opened vials.
Father, hear me now: take me,
leave my mother for the other child.

BONES BE STILL

I see murmuring bones in deep water,
awaiting the final rites to rest.

O undead, fathers' bones,
make the Atlantic your home,

but they wail and curse:

We were sacrificed
to give you life!

Lips remember no songs,
hands no rituals, all I have
are headache dreams.
The sea swells into a hurricane,
the land blackens into cancer,
lightning opens a heart
in the sky, like a boy opening
the window of a hot room
his mother died in.

O undead, why wrath?
I don't know the path.

They answer in thunder:

You ungrateful New World,
too selfish to know the Word.

The Word? I don't know.
The bones stop speaking.

NEW WORLD FRESCOES

I

The gull that bleeds in the Caribbean basin
is the Federation's last emblem put on canvas
by a boy's ratchet-wrists, opening like wings;
then ferns shut on his prodigious task.

Beside him, St Omer sketches the contour
of the peninsula with suffering not present;
his Madonna, a dancing lemon-skin whore,
signed *ad gloriam dei fecit* (that's her scent!),

flourished with coat of arms and his bright motto.
Their master had set them to paint things as they are,
the lesson from Cimabue to Giotto:
always put things down according to nature.
Sifting light, they never imagined his vein
splitting over the archipelago to drain.

II

To paint the great frescoes of the new world,
he uses the woods and the hills for saints,
local dirt unnamed by Adam, its faint,
fecund sex breeding yams; the holy word,

a mitred worm holing to the island's
sulphurous heart where aboriginal deities
sleep another century, worrying volcanologists
who study in mists the peaks of the Pitons.

Like Vulcan, though, his gift is metaphor
beaten into hurricane iambs,

lacking linear elation and science
on canvas. The Prodigal turns to the sea,
to splayed leaves of palms and the surf for
a poetry in which to name each quay.

III

Man's hardest divorce is from the sea.
He hears in the Village's meridian
the sea-lice's dividing eggs, the tree-frogs' plea,
losing their accents to the American

babel, through the amnesic marble arch;
past Garibaldi's half-sheathed sword,
their sounds with fifes and white flags march;
the leading professorial frog bellows, "Words,

you dimwit fireflies, light up History,
for we been in dark now we in New York!"
All in his head, this malarial memory
sickens him, he shivers like a stork;
worse now the bridal sea recedes in foam.
At every corner, leaf-wet whisper, "Go home."

IV

As Boston turns autumn, an American lethargy
haunts the Prodigal on the piazza, waiting
outside the theatre for a young lady
he calls "wheat" for she is everlasting –

something out of Traherne. Fever creeps
in the evening's subterfuge, metallic
sheaves of sidewalk leaves dart and frolic –
are those the tares, and should he now weep?

He does not weep, but takes a narrow
street, where, on one side, a grotesque mural
sheds its skin, revealing pumice stone.
On the other side, a bakery. He sees a sallow
oat-face looking at loaves, their gradual
decline into old age, stale and alone.

V

The cocoa leaves know the name "Tobago",
their speckled light molts his clay-hard body
into another self – the master's shadow
in the house, with a cat, writing everyday.

Poems peel off their barks, the slow flower
in rise each morning, the immortelles' flame
racing to the horizon, winning fame,
hanging his sun-medal gift in the bower.

Paradise was private, except a few tourists
would come and torch themselves on the sand.
The cat yawns behind the glass, flexes its wrists,
then balls into a fist by his writing hand
that lives within the *terza rimas* of stars,
hexameters surge on the grounds of wars.

VI

Here end the works of the sea, the works of love.
— George Seferis

Light breaks the pivot of Roseau Valley
where the Prodigal looks up as an omen-cloud
crawls over Sunday, ending service early.
He shoulders the easel and heads for the road.

After cities and stamp-sized towns in snow,
after the libraries and museums,
the death of friends and their art, he is home
in the valley, his first love. Rain drum

chased the churchgoers to a shelter-
tree. He stares long and hard at them
in white frocks, smiles fresh from the altar.
So easy, he thought, to make their eyes gems.
Or coals. He turns from them to the asphalt,
already ablaze, steaming with water and salt.

AT BAY

When I say "coffee",
she thinks Cavafy,
and my head turns to marble.

Sometimes, "sea frisk",
means Seferis —
she is that galvanized.

Those two old friends,
Cavafy and Seferis,
had one secret

that is not the musk
of cut flowers or ancient papyrus,
musty in clay jars;

no, she says laughing,
it's history and mystery,
the Janus of genius —

not our genius, mind you,
but theirs; coffee mouth
Cavafy and sea-frisky Seferis,

themselves not lovers,
just timeless and youthful,
fleshed into marble busts,

left on a hot terrace,
sunbathing and overlooking
the vacant bay,

where startled umbrellas
open to the spectrum
of the light's aging.

ERRANT

Eyesight good for the devil, his kingdom
made out of insects' parts in a dim room,
a curtain hitched in the window like a tomb-
stone. Woodworms tick shovels in the crossbeams;
coal-written signs hieroglyphed the wall; the town's
one necromancer shuffles up and mutters
what his hand touches: a lethal science.
Outside, the house has other warnings: a ram's
skin, its skull and horns nailed to the doorway.

Vine-choked veranda, root-split steps cut off
by a cesspool – alive and dead in it –
cricket balls and our eyes peering at this dark fortress.

This time I am to fetch it, the last leather
ball to fly over the fence like a black butterfly;
and at that age, oblivion matters, so one boy
at a time is sacrificed. The evening too early
to declare "bad light", I push my head between
the barbwire, crossing over, laughter like goats.

A SMALL PANTHEON

Horace

My cousin, born February,
can't read this apology signed
with two fishes: sorry for feeding you
the poison bread, a Roman deed.
Piscis Austrinus, you will meet
a water-bearer, sent to wash your feet,
she will dry them with her head cloth,
hold you like a mother – be her son,
cousin, so you will never want
for love, or feast, and you will learn
words for your hurt, to no longer
wonder at a coin's face.

Rosemary

The woodcutter's wife – sawdust hair –
I remember her footprints entering the grove;
I touched her and the beach shuddered.
I wanted to marry her on the leaves,
but the sky reflected in her eyes,
and I caught the silver glimpse of a far
jet, its engine thundered above the surf's
breath. She pulled her blouse over her head
and her words splintered finer and finer
in the plane's curling echo.

Floyd

Orthodox in daylight, at nightfall
this proselyte was the clean-shaved
emperor of Caesar's Go-Go Club,
star boy in his shiny shirt. His hands
greased mammoth collection plates
thrust into his face, pinky gold ring
glinting with their bosoms' sheen.
In the half-shadow, in the scent of burnt
butts, processed hair, rummy lipstick,
an olive-branch sweat branded
his forehead. In the heave of bass-
line, he sank low in the leather sofa,
ears thudding, a holy flock
of doves in his head.

Ezekiel

Seer of stones, madman praising
the sun in treetops, he cursed
the barbwire horizon and the three-wire
poles planted through his bush path.
I passed him there in his squalor,
son of Buzi in Babylon, vines rusting
on his head, two deserts for eyes,
soles parched where he sought salt
from the earth, walking
the full circle of the district.
Power cut nights, I heard his torn
voice from the Pentecostal hills,
singing us to sleep, singing:
When the roll when the roll
when the roll is called up yonder...

FAR DISTRICT

i/ Outer Eden

When nothing existed in the district
and I walked around with knapsack and notebook,
like Adam in the garden, naming things,

a derelict at Half Way Tree Square told me
the sea is our genesis and the horizon, exodus.
I wanted to recant, "There is nothing here,

no visible history." My tongue stoned,
dried-brain, I boarded the sardine-can bus
to school. Packed in that heat, a memory

sparked and died in the murmur of tired bodies.
I limboed between the aqueducts and poui trees
on campus before History, the histrionic

ghost staring at the blackboard, at centuries
chalked in white like the professor's hair,
his liver-spotted hand holding the ruler,

stabbing timelines, then stopping at 1492.
"Before that date, nothing. A less barbaric
term, a civil one in light of the tropic – I mean

topic – is an *area of darkness.* A few primal
inventions; tools fashioned from bones and stones,
but no real industry there, until sugar."

He meant that shit hole east of Portland,
Outer Eden. Back there calendar was useless.
I knew days by studying the sugar-cane cutters:

Monday a trickle, Tuesday a drove,
Wednesday and Thursday, a river swell
that on payday-Friday flooded the town square.

Sunday mornings I knew by two happenings.
First the lashing of Cre-Cre's albino woman
by Cre-Cre before the first cock crowed,

and then before church time, that perennial hog,
Hyacinth, shuffling yard-to-yard, hawking
her dry goods. Today, Friday, if I leave

this lecture and go back, the talks wouldn't
be *Niña*, *Pinta* and *Santa Maria* –
not those nothings – but how nothing happens there.

And I'd hiss my teeth; stasis in any name is stasis.
That benign parish is the heart's dark interior,
the island's bushed-in mindset, a place

forgotten by the cartographer,
but buried inside me to decompose.
Here I am, planted in this desk

of a nascent history, and it dawned
that the mad, hermeneutic Rasta
was wrong; my beginning was not the sea,

my departure not the horizon:
I am nothing, I am dirt, where no light
can reach. There this monody I unearthed.

Early on the white marl road I met Cre-Cre,
cut-off khaki gripping his cedar thighs.
Frightened, not of him, but my own scrawny

self forbidden to go river. Suspicious, he asked,
"Boy, your mother chain you to books. You ever go river?"
Just us standing on that dazzling road.

"Out there is just one man with him God,
and though I beat that woman for nothing,
He pass no judgment in me wooden boat."

*

I know rivers the way I know hate.
From the stygian bank silver-swirling,
birthing night blacker than my mother's skin,

I found myself one night at the swamp,
two worn coins for the boater, dumb
like the moon ownself when he pushed off.

We went silent, till deeper we came
to a spot of wailing women, their hair torn.
At this branch of shrieking, I bawled out,

"What wrong with all a you, eh?"
But the hushed boater rounded a bend,
the river changed into lapis lazuli

that soon as I saw it, pain knifed me,
pain in the joints, and I lay stiff on the skiff,
whispering *woi woi woi* and didn't see

everything brighten to crackling stars.
Then I felt a scorch and cold sweat started
to wash me, and I shivered in heat.

Dark covered me and I slept.
Is like that one time over at Navy Island,
twilight turning on the harbour lights,

I closed my eyes on my back on a raft,
and drifted, spliff smoke carried me
into a gelid dream. I woke centuries

after (or before), in a forest. My limbs
were the leopard's, camouflaged in dry
grass; my name was not nothing,

but a breeze blew the grass, turned the raft
over into the sea. Half drowned,
I scrambled to land. I didn't learn my name.

iii/ Gilbert

After the hurricane, mud filled the streets.
People believed it to be the end: no
banana tree survived the breeze's slaughter,

fish pots blown away, staggering children
walked around debris all day, combing for
what adults missed. I remembered little.

My grandma had huddled the family in,
boiled dumplings, filled us and stored us under beds.
Coming out, the yard unrecognizable,

an uncle cursed, "But rass, God nuh easy."
Grandma shot him a look that shut him down.
"Thank Father God, the house strong like the ark."

We found the crab-shell school broken,
playground mangled, spiked with zinc and steel
we picked through. Nothing was salvaged.

A few days later, a government van,
with a cheeky brown man who roamed with us.
"This parish is the worse. How people live so?"

He brought out surveying instruments, we crowded
and he shooed us, repeating, "Official business"
until hoarse. He didn't stay the whole day.

One night my uncle told me the man's finding.
The whole thing didn't make sense.
"I tell you boy, God forgot us. Sleep now."

*

After all that ravish, no power was left
in the land for days. On a calabash
moonnight, revivalists came to the square

for our souls. The rum drinkers and whores
of payday Fridays turned sudden believers.
Mother, a reluctant saint, brought me there.

Candles bled on a white and red tablecloth,
moths dying in wax. Frenzied women swayed
behind a tall man, head wrapped in turban.

He clutched and waved the Bible at us.
"The land, the land, witnesses, is cursed.
All you here, staring like motherless calfs

are wicked, that's why God strike we bad bad."
The clump of teeth shone false. "No little grace,
no little God no day; all manner a evil isms:

alcoholism, whorism and heathenism."
Underneath the light post without light,
I watched a wail erupt in the crowd.

"What kind of place this? All you shame me."
Shame him? Man, it stuck me and I wanted
to break the crowd, turn and face them:

"Know what this is? Let me tell all you here.
From Duckenfield to Dalvey to Cheswick,
and all the other back-of-bush district them,

all this is nothing, you hear? Nobody knows
nor care about all you poor and black,
all you cane cutters and yam planters.

And I sick of it to rass. Everything
here a backside waste of time, from that jungle
school to that jungle post office, all joke."

I leaned on the light post without light, sweating.
Shivers going through all of them. I made to move,
then, like a match strike, power came back.

iv/ The visitors

The day yawned wide like a caesura.
I came across a fallen cedar
at the edge of a valley, two mongrels

34

latched on the asphalt. John crows
circled my vision. I put my hands
in my coconut-husk head, tangled bristles

winced. Nothing trudged up the road.
Mongrels parted, gone. Then out of the heat,
wavered two boys, like a moving mirage,

squealing and pointing behind them
at two jeeps in the distance. The asphalt
trembled and whispered under my feet.

They cut past, invincible beasts on prey,
carrying behind them a throng of faces.
One hailed me, just his neck craning back:

"Oui there, Bird Boy, you not coming to square?"
He vanished; another finished: " 'Mericans, boy.
Big flim people them, sir. Them say we must come."

I stared after him with not a word for the
bewildered sweat in my palms.
One last boy wobbled up, buried the hatchet:

"Yes man, hottaclaps in the place for true!
I'm a star-boy, you know. Big big time, man!
Like Clint Eastwood and all them. So, you coming?"

*

We swarmed the camera crew,
jaundiced jesuses
giving us candies on cue.

We'd never seen white
skin this close
and could smell it right –

it smell full of money,
sweet Yankee dollars.
"Tek me nuh honey,

see some pum-pum here."
Circle-eyed gods clicked,
a child flicked there

and became a star.
Through the barracks,
snapping charred

verandas and outside bathrooms,
we followed and gathered around,
wowed when they wowed at our tombs:

"Hey man, this shit's amazing!"
The factory's churning chimneys,
little exclamation marks fuming,

captured his attention.
The cameras turned from us
and winked at the scrap iron.

The cyclop-gods struck
and struck Tropicana
until the work whistle blew (*Oh fuck!*)

We slinked back to work –
donkeys to cane fields,
jackasses in factory shirts

to the mill. They mounted Rovers,
riding shot-gun, leaving hot dust
in the town square to hover.

v/ District Triptych

1: Tropicana Sugar Estate

It sat fuming in the middle of town,
mechanic heart shunting day into night.
Tractors of us, hallowed eyes, begging

to worship in its slaked lime, in its oil
and tar. The molasses dumped in our chests,
mixed in our school milk, and round buns

we ate, until we grew strong enough to cut
the canes, load them on the tractors,
grind them in the mill, into crystallized

sugar – that we never tasted – too dear
for our pockets, so we drank our tea bitter,
to purge our blood, to not murder the boss

each fortnight when the pay came up short
after carrying the sack of sun on our backs –
he laughed and the rum fired us

to the haberdashery square, strung with soundboxes,
to dance and flirt, to piss and scream hate,
to wallow in dirt, to beat our women,

cuss coolies, until Sunday, sabbath,
gripped the district into a petulant silence,
pockets empty in the pews, our eyes trailing ants.

2: Prudence

Tropicana first, then whores.
            — *Edict*

She was the only speckled-skin whore in Duckenfield,
you'd have to pay real copper to drink her browning —
good hair — a talcum-star blazoned on her chest.

Evenings, on the way from primary school,
I saw her, dressed in cowgirl boots and cutoffs,
blouse opened on a barstool outside *The Cool Spot*,

fanning herself. Men in factory uniforms
and cane-black suits talked all at once to her.
She'd kick out her boots when touched,

scattering them like fowls, bickering and fighting.
They'd cool down, regroup, talking smooth,
buying her drinks. She never spoke, only smiled.

Sometimes, she'd walk away with one. One evening,
she waved at me from her perch. The day felt strange:
she wasn't a whore, but a bronze goddess

with the powdered star of my passion,
though I was too young to serve, (but soon).
After that evening I walked by the bar

in slow motion, watching her long, sad face,
wishing to be old, waiting for my wave.
It never came; her star faded.

She was stabbed in a bar in Kingston.
Only men attended her funeral, extra drunk.
I watched her hands in the casket.

3: Tribune of Old Men at the *Cool Spot Tree*

Outside HARRIS' FURNITURE STORE, the aged
and the aging, glued to tree stumps, sculpted
indelibly to nailed-up domino tables, held council.

Mornings I cruised their ken, khaki pressed stiff
off mother's iron glare, slackened by evening
with the tile-wisdoms they'd throw at me.

Prudence, guest of honour on the bamboo
bench, listened to their bagasse brags, paunch belly
lies growling off rum-slick tongues, muffled

by tractors packed with canes to Tropicana.
Mouths opened like ackee:
                              "Now this Castro
is a true general. I respect him."

"Is my pardner that, boy!"
                              Meaning the man
across the table and the don hour-and-half
by boat, clenched like a cigar between us

and US: "I ca'an wait
for him to free up more powder."
"You hear 'bout all them boy who find barrels
                    at Holland Bay?"

"They pick the shit up like stones and shells."
One pounded the table:
                              "Is only say we government a romp."
Another: "Them to legalize the weed, take we out a bondage."

His face grew a creased and distant red
clay – lethargic as the donkey passing,
amnesiac grass bundled on its back.

Bondage was more than the one-room police
station, bars rustier than the corporal's suit.
And it not only mean black man in chains

shown on TV February time; bondage
was all them shacks in malarial gullies –
is that word teacher used other day: *poverty*.

Teacher say poverty is what breeding crime
("True, but a whole lot more breeding," they laughed),
and is why so much badman Rhygins

taking the island for the OK Corral
and *The Harder They Come*. Too long silent,
they shuffled the tiles. It was dusk already.

vi/ Branch of Shrieking

Her hardboiled eyes followed me around
the room, specs weighing her nose bridge,
missing nothing as I walked the shelves'

dusty volumes. You'd have missed the place,
smacked between the barracks and rum bars;
burnt cane-ash and marl-dust covered any signs

the district had a library, tomb-quiet,
except for the rusty fan stirring dim light
and shadow. My eyes strained to catch

what was inscribed on the books' spines
below the film of dust. Astigmatic,
my asthma lungs lurched at a discovery:

Stevenson's *Treasure Island* and Defoe's *Crusoe*.
From that evening, and many evenings,
I was Jim Hawkins of the towns.

Days wore on, and a Crusoe melancholy
sunk in. *I looked now upon the world
as a thing remote, which I had nothing*

to do with rang my head when I returned.
Her shrivelled black hands grabbed mine.
I yelled: "I had nothing to do with it, at all."

*

Then, one night, a shriek catapulted across
the sleeping district, sending the bush brigade
in a sandfly-panic to the standpipe.

When the hysteria calmed into morning,
it was discovered that it was not
Tropicana that caught fire; they sighed off.

I stood for a while as they brushed past.
"Nothing more than that librarian did it."
"What a rass if it was the factory, eh boy?"

I stood until day lighted, and as I turned,
walking on the rubble, I saw Bogle.
He looked around as freed slaves,

Baptist Christians from Stony Gut, gathered.
A cloudburst. They evaporated. The cane field
grew green. Rain drowned the burnt books.

*

Above coconut trees, lit like torches,
a single sun rotted everything below.
Potbellied, gutter-mouth pickney

attacked a wild hog, mother turned back
to her pot cooking on Bible leaves.
I watched, a sandfly of the landscape.

Tropicana whistle blew, ended daylight.
I felt myself graduating from the trees,
something thundering in my head.

vii/ Passage to Portland

Golden Grove, the rim of Outer Eden.
No gold paved the potholed road
out of the district. I looked down at them

gathering in the early light, long-suffering
market women bundling at the bus stop,
silent as yams on their crocus-laden tie-heads.

A backfire forewarned a red behemoth
creeping up the road, in white-hot letters
on the windscreen, *Illustrious Rat Fink,*

and on its side, *K Sons.* "Boy, you deaf ears?
I say to help me load in me things them.
And why it look like you bawling? Portland

is paradise, you know. Not a thing
to miss here." Her face a withered orange.
"It have beach and tourist. You the boy

42

who got scholarship for school there?"
I nodded.

         "Do good good, me son."

Packed in, the driver cranked the engine,
adjusted his marine goggles and blasted the horn.
The next time I was able to lift my head

I saw for the first time, through a chip
in the roadside bushes, the open sea,
crossed and recrossed by sunbeams.

The bus stammered around a final corner.
The notebook dampened under my palms.
I looked in the rearview for a flaming sword.

DARKNESS EVERYWHERE

Even now in that drizzled-out town,
posts without lights are mounted.
At six pm all doors are bolted, a pail
of enamel water placed in the living room.
Talk is kept low, not a single call answered,
and if the third call is in the voice of a woman,
the bed is turned, toe to head, head to toe.

Even now in the hills, under low stars,
Kumina drummers beat the goatskin
drums in the clearing, dancers in white
and red circle, sweat frocks wheeling
to the katta sticks and shac-shacs, until
a woman froths into spirit, and a shiny
grapefruit-mouth man, face dark in the torch's
flame, sprays rum in her eyes and on the dirt.

Below this, in a tenement yard, moth-men
gather at the candle of a domino table,
silent in the warmth of their skins.
One, Boy-Boy, stares dull, waiting to bow
the final piece in the constellation,
his eyes follow the dirty tiles, blackened nails
scratch his forehead, knowing any moment
now – then *bam!* he shatters the table with one
strike. They cheer and swiftly reshuffle the stars,
share and begin the pattern the same.

In a backroom, the men dimming
into their game, wax eyelids slowing down,
a mother puts on her nightie and lies beside
her son, whispering a guard for his dream,

that no rolling-calf's ball and chain steals
him to the valley. She then blows out
the oil lamp, falling darkness everywhere,
plunging the room and the hills into one.

BAM-BAM

make thee an ark of gopher wood

After school we'd stone him from running distance,
flinging and yelling, *Maggot-brain, donkey-cock madman.*
When a stone hit his penis, the hitter victory danced,
and we'd crowd around screaming, *Target to rass, man!*
Saturdays and Sundays we'd never see him and I'd never thought
to see him one Saturday afternoon, naked, in my lane, outside my gate.

He carried nothing other than his matted head, his mud crusting skin,
yet I feared him to death as how I feared church; my tongue pebbled;
he shuffled through the gate, talking as he approached,

> *The whole earth is here*
> *all the arks are here, we stone the arks and poison food,*
> *you listen mosquito, boy, or you bite them and eat?*
> *Stone fly from your hand and you feel you is man,*
> *well, I am at heaven gate with a light on me tongue,*
> *a bulb, an electric bulb, shocking the ark to life.*
> *Zzzzzzzzzzzzzzzzz, mosquito, zzzzzzzzzzzzzzzzzzzzzz,*
> *you listening, right, or you in the flood, ark?*
> *All God's children is ark, bird in hand of the man*
> *and now the whole earth is here, all the arks.*

The gate banged, leaving a rock pitching against my skull,
I felt the light going out of the day, and a grey,
lowering itself, covered all as far as I could see.

THE VENUS OF WILLENDORF

Immodest in broad daylight,
a ruddy-bellied woman bathes
at the public stand-pipe,
jubilant with water laughter
as we all stand and wait
with our buckets and bottles.
No one dares advance
an "Excuse me, miss."
Rather, we watch soap foams
in her creases then, washed out
clean and black, she shines
like a new tyre tube.
The pipe runs on high,
a stream forms around
her tiny ankles, hidden
like stones or a boy's marbles.
Not until she is fully dried,
her coarse hair brushed
violently to release water,
and her rag wrung twice,
does she step from the trough,
timidly balancing on
one foot while drying the other,
then shoves it in a push-toe
rubber slipper – she repeats
this, laughing, "O, Jesus, my body!"
Clean as a pimento tree
after rain, she gathers her pans,
paying us no mind, whistles home.

WALKING WITH ATLAS

We took the short drive out of the city,
to the fish market in the early morning,
sleepless vendors waving us to their goods.
The bright fins dazzled in the baskets,
and the near sea, shined clean
by the hands of the scaling women,
purified with lime after being gutted by fishermen,
idled in the warmth, as if never touched.

They saw we were not quick to purchase
and preferred to walk with the slow dogs,
stopping to nose the fresh blood and salt
in the stalls, their life's work, the sticks
worn by breeze and years left in the open
to the sun and rain, their own sudden,
changing tempers. We picked through gaulins
squabbling over garbage that lined the shore.

"They need security guards here," my brother
remarked, his one day out of uniform,
and I thought his face darkened in the scar-
let light, but he laughed and punched my shoulder.
We were at the last stall. The world didn't
totter; the sea stayed in balance, stretching
miles, calm and reticent how he framed it.
We returned and bought snappers wrapped in leaves.

PENALTY SHOT

Then there was this boy who rafted to school,
his dad a dark profile in cold morning air,
lean and curved, as we gathered on the peninsula
for early devotions, the punctual light crossing
the battlement; we answered "present" or "absent"
to names shouted, fidgeting in our class lines.

Quiet boy, khaki pants rolled up, smelling of fish
scales and lime. Christ, he could strike the football
like a killer, but we were all animals on the playfield,
and when we ran out of nicknames for him,
he became *No Name Boy*, because he didn't
talk much, and never challenged the names we gave.

When the sea swallowed going-home bells,
we rushed hell-loose to the bus stop, firing insults
and next-day's war threats, but he walked slowly,
turning at the cliff's gate, stopping to roll up his pants.
I shouted to him one evening as he got down
on his knee: "School tomorrow?" He looked through

the right angles of his leg, certain I didn't know
his name. A strange thing passed between us,
a bent ball, skidding towards the two open posts,
and there I was in the clearing, no defenders,
but I stalled at the shot, until now I recall
his real name, in the jerk of memory's net: Eusebius Titus.

DORIS AT THE RIVER

There, on the pendent boughs her coronet weeds
Clambering to hang, an envious sliver broke.
                    — Shakespeare, *Hamlet*

Her melody broke through a shell
over the town that August we found
her in the arms of native Ariel,
strands of hair and leaves in her mouth.

Who knew she lived in such troubled
branches, in the corners of daydreams,
singing the perfect epitaph:
All things that you possess, possess their death.

The river streaked into a brown mirror,
the tail of her slime-green dress brushed
fallen woods in decay as we pulled her out.
Her hands were clasped on her chest.

This was the work of devotion,
not art — the silver of love, cracked.
Ants draped her eyelids, indifferent
to the sun and us staring down.

THE BAUBLE-WORLD

In winter, her visage was my vase
when the animals claimed the city
from the reptilian water sewer.
My head shrunk into a spit-blue sea,
with twisted-up pear grove, fishing boats
parked like yellow cabs, the sun rotated
a rimless tyre black kids jump through,
to skid bare-assed into a life of misfortunes.
I landed here, on cold ground,
bewildered by the solstice, hanging
a coat on my frame to remember
life upon Setebos, the time spent
eyeing Miranda from a dim cornea,
her face shining with hibiscus sweat,
her ankles sandy before the dive,
her tongue petalling when she hissed,
her nostrils flaring into pink holes
as I handed her the promise ring.
She broke the vine, left me stooged
for this sour-mouth, sore-foot boy,
sworn to his bow and my girl.
I tied him to a post in an ant nest,
and chanted: "Mooncalf,

        mooncalf,

               you can't walk?"
The boy changed skin to rass,
last time I saw him, tall in a suit,
she was his bride. "So you married?"
She spat:
     "Yes. Wha'ppen to that?"
I made to say, fuck-off, Mira –
but Mooncalf pirouetted up
and took her away. The crippled fuck.
I hobbled home to pack my bags.

[Exeunt, fades to Mona. Poui trees in bloom]

At orientation, the blind boy of Attica
asked: "So what country crotches like, man?"
His name was Cyco.
     "Soft, like ripe naseberry."
He laughed: "Boy, you a poet for real!"
No, Cyclops, poets are unreal.
He batted off down the hall, deejaying
something I couldn't hear, I stood
grudging whatever light carried him.
One night, after the hard-wine bacchanal,
I woke to piss over the balcony in the garden,
I looked down and saw him, walking stick
held up in the moonlight, waving and waving.
He turned to me, face blank as a paved road:
"Poet, what you doing?
     Mind you piss on me!"
Hands froze on my cock. He said, looking up:
"In the land of the seeing blind,
     the real bat is king,
and he lives by driving his beasts
     under the sun.
For mine the Kingdom, the Power and Glory."
He moved off into the dark.
     "Don't envy me;
the weight of ascended things is heavy."

I told him that the effeminate professor
unnerves me during Conrad – the dainty
hair toss, big soft hands wiping sweat,
lips smacking: "Mistah Kurtz, he dead."
What horror, nailing the neocolonial God
across iron board islands, the shadowy heart,
like St Thomas, a thick humus in my throat.
I also asked: "What's more elegiac than history?"

52

He replied, as if I was blind:
                    "Love."
After class I walked to the aqueducts.
Ruined stone arches, the slave water
dried into mulching leaves, the orange bricks
almost dust. I felt the unrequited flames
in their granite hearts disintegrating under my gaze.
The sun wanted to set, but the empire
wouldn't let it. A bird shat on my arm —
its idea of *oriens ex occidente lux*. My eyes caught
it going east, to New York. I followed.

MONTALE'S LEMONS

My first snow, I open the pages
of Montale, the scent of iron
and light coming out of heads

of lemon trees in the middle
of an orchard where raucous boys
play, not hearing the eel-quiet laureate

who roams under a sky dappled with rust.
He comes through the gate, plucks
acanthus, unburdening himself of the city

and the classics left in his study.
Standing still, his shadow moves
to branches brushing earth,

freckling it with flame. Montale stoops
in flecked leaves to a flickering secret,
and what could be translated

as winter fixes a spire in my chest
and my eyes go low down
with that crouching tower;

I cling to a still revolving truth:
the world is a golden calyx,
but home is a burst lemon,

a child weeping at the cane root.

LETTER FROM HOME

In this Brooklyn room, in the dead
of winter, as they say, opening
a tangerine's heart, the room glows,
and her letter sighs open, phrases imitating
spiky ice trees outside, hiding handbells,
their block procession harking: Spring.
Sentences set down dearly,
with tenderfoot ease, alert to the forest,
she warns:
    Concentrated effort
of writing poetry is a spiritual activity
which makes one completely forget,
for the time being, that one has a body.

Lady, my body has forgotten me,
in the hunger for words,
at my anchorite desk, where I bloom
into the night cereus, newly repeated
and profoundly each time.

I break for a tangerine's peg,
its citrus cracks the cold, blood
regains circuit, my fingers twitch
into legs crossing the field, into
a bookshelf, up the living spines
and the brook-frozen names
never to be reborn on the fawn's brown coat.

Her scrawl again – *I am very old* – multiplying
weak lines, binding an anchor of primeval
sensations, and I too have aged in this weather,
far from home's vein orange. O vanity!

She ends: *How an old person will envy you*
your world full of inspiration,
                                    and at that summit
of love, springing from wherever she writes,
she forgets to sign her name, but bless her
shaky hand, her T's crucified in black ink,
her withered O's mouth, a skinned-cold
fruit, warmed in my palms – bless the snow
that blinds me, the sun imprisoned in the heater;
bless the frosted glass panes memory
rubs up against, through which I look
and sneeze, shaking icicles onto the page.

ICARUS AFTER

When grief strikes in the house,
open the sea Ariel protects,
stitch glowworms in book spines,
give an ear to Thelonius, a sparrow

in your lap. Among the city's
mannequins, someone touches your coat,
and a leaf falls on a park bench,
ending autumn early. In your house

with the horse's exposed anatomy,
a chestnut-flamed glass on the table,
the East River is here, lending her
veil to your ship in the fog.

What the twilight does not say
you have said with surgical ease:
the spangled scars we wear
are scratches on the landing.

AUTOBIOGRAPHY OF SNOW

for Claude McKay, 1889 – 1948

Grey statues stand
> *with pigeons' hearts*
children's calls and cries
> *rustle in treetops*
bear-heavy women trot
> *with heads low*
white aliveness
> *coming out of them.*

I come, Claude, in a warm October
and watch boys at the rim of a fountain.
A sun-coloured ball floats past the ukulele man,
past hula-hoop-girls, twirling sunlight.
The juggler spins eyeballs through O-O
brass rings. A child lolls in its stroller,
lovers kiss and part underneath the arch.

*

Drizzle above the high-rises.
Through the street, coats swish by;
black boots clomp into a coffee shop.
Nina Simone pours pastel blues –
I know *this*; a finger of memory
lifts to the waitress and to forecast
the rain back home. Remember island rain,
Claude? Grass and asphalt blending,
the road a crucible, even the dog-shit
smells good, even the hot cane field?

She takes the signal,
brings us two steaming cups.
You take off, Harlem or Russia. Doesn't matter.

Now is right – my status alien – to weigh my lines.
Most are antique, and have entered antiquity
with my slow pace. In my coffee a hurricane is brewing.

I rise and tip her well.
Outside, the street evaporates.

*

> Lorca's dead body
> > stalks these parks
> with yours I pass
> > my shoulders
> tucked neat in song
> > quick into the queue
> going underground
> > my mind sings:

tonight! tonight!

I must bear my navel-string in this city,
heavy with snow, the American fiction,
bogus dreams that put us on ice.
I know snow as soap opera, the comedy
of white heap shovelled into strophe
and anti-strophe for long blocks – snow
as envy, a shaken blanket making a lasting
echo over clean avenues. O Flame-heart,
I stay within the middle of dark passages,
roads sliced into trails going nowhere,
waiting for your coat to turn the corner,
licked by a lamp's flame – the fire between
Christ's palms. Back in the apartment's
hole I bury my hands in this frigid craft,
and tremble, McKay, husking a way home.

VINTAGE RAIN

For there was no rain in Paradise
because of the delicate construction
of the spiritual herbs and flowers.
— Christopher Smart

I read your hornbook in the after calm
of the hurricane staggering off to Cuba,
hurling at the door, pounding the window.
The bars in your book kept it out.

The cat's eyes and electric skin gave off light
when the generator died; the district charged
with a drunken rage, mouths gaped
silver at the storm-face moon, holding up

a cyclops-eye. Gauze of rain drizzled
apologies in the valley, not the early lances
flung in the hill's head, a head full
of noises, but a hum, slowing the night.

I considered the cat and myself in the echo
of the conquistador's lightning, visor lowered
somewhere in the gulf stream. Then, master,
you stepped from your mad cell

into my rattled room of torn cobwebs,
your hair thunder, cat musk and angel tiger
scent on your clothes. You've escaped your century's
confinement, in the haze of rain. How?

"By raising my book's canticle in the storm,
I heard the harp and the bees' concentric
melody called me from a hard night,
to bear the fruits to end your suffering."

The rain, heavier than flowers,
lowered cloud-berries between us, and
then stopped. My eyes adjusted to him.
I shivered with the first bite.

PROMETHEUS

He was a parhelion cutting
across the night avenue, something
weighting his hips like stones.

You came up next, face melting
off windscreens, a tree blown
leafless and a goat herder

climbed down from the constellation
with salt on his tongue
and something in his waist.

Then the goats with fennel-stalks
in their mouths packed the street
ruminating their tedious tales.

Across the stream of them
he mouthed to you something
swallowed in bleats.

Staggering forward, you shouted
What, man, what!
But a gadfly got loose in the lot.

Stampede swirled war wind;
half blinded, you looked up, and saw
a great eagle lifting him off.

APRIL

I often recall in the month of April,
the Hebrew girl I sheltered the storm with alone.
She taught me that the wayside church
was a shell of her love, empty and full of rain.

When I said, "Lets climb the belfry,"
the host in her hair nodded, her pearl body
incised the night into another wisdom:
the four hundred and forty years away

into the wilderness — wet wood and wet cobweb.
In the damp darkness, we shivered at the nearness
of water-stained stars, and the distant hills,
hunched like camped pilgrims in cloaks.

She cried, "There is Chanah Ruth and her children."
I saw only the black rain on black heads, herded
above a white stone ridge. She spoke into me crystals,
"My mothers are nothing but well-placed rubble."

So are mine. Her words said in April, lowered now
in the trees of May, my head hanging over Buber's
terrific revelation: *So, waiting, I have won from
you the end.* Maybe not the end, but the breaking off.

TWO TREES

She would announce from her yard
before one dropped, sending us in a flurry
through the fence under the mango tree,
heads up for the blind fruit that would come
tearing down the branches. Falling on knees,
we would go helter-skelter in the grass, until someone
lifted the yellow trophy high before running off,
teeth peeling the skin off the furry flesh.

Other times we would try to sneak past
her perennial stare on the other tree.
She would catch us, and Kumina-talk: "Oui, kinte
pan you malu and tek back a boi fi me."
And we would bring her "boi", the cigarette
she would light and smoke backwards,
sticking out an ash tongue before spitting
butt and phlegm at our toes. She would go on:
"Before the sea tek Gabby, I know;
I sit right here, to rass, and feel sand
in my ears. I feel my belly bottom sinking.

Then when my son Baba come tell me
him drown, I see him leaning on the nutmeg tree,
and I say, 'Gabby, you not coming in?'
Him smile, blowing short, bubbles
just a bust in him mouth. Could the man move?
No sir, him still like stone. Him right there,"
she would then point at the spotted tree,
blighted corneas thick and white on it,
"telling me when mango going to fall."

UNDERGOD

I stepped from bar to pavement at Bleecker Street,
and entered a Diwali. Provincial
in background, I startled rat to subway;
as I descended, a nightstick was beating
the daylights out of a black kid.

I tipped turnstile Charon his $2.00;
deep in a bench, underground pulsing, I waited.
Two years ago there were no subways, a beachhead
defended by sand-flies, keeping America
at bay one suck at a time, before seasonal storms

wiped it clean. In 1507, my prone
acre couldn't fit on Martin Waldseemüller's
Universalis Cosmographia, but christened
through that chattel link, an outpost for the Common-
wealth, islands baptized in the triangular trade.

I sat underneath the world and it appeared
nothing here has its first name; Tainos called us
Xaymaca, a sound like coco pods opening:
the "land of wood and water". Further north
of that origin, punch-drunk in the shadows,

I didn't hear, not a peep from the old rat,
the pigs in blue, their steel badges shone
the light of empire, and before my rights
could be read, I kissed their polished boots.
Inert on my knees, bloodied, I tried my voice:

"I am Madiba... no, I am Kondo...no...no...Ion
of Asante... no, sir... it is Yoruba... Zulu!"
Nothing registered in the flashlights' hot bulbs.
Keys rattled like manacles, the train pulled in.
They ringed my wrists with steely bracelets again.

TERMINUS

I

I didn't recognize the mountain
as the plane touched down,
a chunk of it given over
to some obscure industry.
I've returned to the dirt of home,
because of death, to bear the casket,
and face their questions, to depart again.
The island glittered from the air
before the craft dropped, rust zinc
appeared, perishing under the sun.
Passengers streamed from the iron hull
to the first stab of sunlight. Memory
salted, the wounds healed away,
but here, by the sea, grew raw again.
I stared over the heads in line
of that slow moving perdition,
and heard a tractor clawing
out the mountain; my heart harrowed,
for I swore at the stamp-in desk,
stood my father, almost alive, waiting.

II

Imagine Mandelstam barefoot
on the rabid streets of Russia,
and whisper, "The bread of poetry
is coarse; this is a tough life."
It cannot be enough not to suffer
with words, a syllable sole-worn to prove
nothing except the shape of ache,
tortured thoughts, the small things,
the dusty aspirations gathered after sleep.

My dry lips break and crease
with unfulfilled lines, the copper tongue
stalls shut into its dark hole.
Say anything, and nothing happens.

III

That time father came back from the cold
was my first time at the airport.
The silent uncle drove, and I was ignited,
watching the moving world:
trees turned into light-posts, mountains levelled,
and when the car picked up speed on the last
strip to the NMIA, like a gull going
for the kill, my first plane!, swift
and gentle, touched down, out of sight,
then another, Phoenix, up and away.
It was night but all the lights made it daylike
as the car throttled in the waiting, the uncle
so silent except his breath rising and dying
in the front seat. He broke his sabbatical,
"See him there," and I turned
to my life's dilemma,
mistaking every stranger for him at every port
of entry and exit, wild-eyed
at the scattering of arrivals, searching out
his face at the edge of the terminal.

BRYAN'S BAY REVISITED

It was this beach, a rub-a-dub summer
night, the day-torched sand trampled
into a holy ground of bare feet, in the sultry
scent of herb smoke and roasted peanuts,
my father clung cool-and-deadly to my mother
in a haul-and-pull dance, the first time they met,
not easing off to take a piss or point fingers
at the sky, luminous with gun salutes.
They ended up in his beach-shanty, holey boards
stuffed with sand grains and newspapers.

It is an empty arena today, the fugitive sun
ramboes across the sky, and in the near horizon,
my father is falling into its arc, a buoy bobbing
like a woman forgotten on the dance floor,
sand on her heels, music slapping the leaves
of her hair, and as the breeze combs through mine,
I take off in one brisk gallop into the sea's mouth,
sucking salt of all I know of the sea, of her wide
skirt, the holes of his merino straining red, gold,
and green, the hot spokes of their love, broken, turn.

BACK TO THE BRANCH

Too much of water hast thou, poor Ophelia.
— Shakespeare, *Hamlet*

I read her face by kerosene light
when I opened the door and saw her naked,
her hair wet with dew and the moon.

She cried: *Father, you freed me,*
but made me your sweet votive piece,
your plaything. I invited her in and boiled

the bitter tea leaves I knew.
She curled on the sofa as night
passed, talking into the cushion:

I have fallen Father, for you;
everyday in the Law Hall,
the "seething authorities"

stare me down, their whispers curdle
around me. I am a terrible fish
that can't go back to the branch,

because I am stripped of my virgin's
veil. Yes, we know what we are,
but know not what we may be. God,

the dark outside! Your lamp so bright —
I saw from the road its flame
and knew you would take me again.

Here I am, my spirit left in a ditch,
but here — she placed my hand
on her damp blouse — *have the rest.*

NANA

1/ Lifting of the Veil

Necromancy is Duckenfield;
everything there is about spirits,
midnight chains pulled by cows,
unholy symbols in the sky,
or across the forehead of a village boy.
There the unflinching romance
of the religious and the profane:
pastor's daughter turned whore, burning
crosses and sleeping with black heart men.

On the edge of this swamp district,
Nana was born, daughter of the barefoot
poet who walks around with his sweat-stained
voice, declaring the Apoplectic End,
and her mother, the silent black
woman who wears pencils in a red turban,
scratching the dust with a fowl's feather.

A blood wail blasts the night
of her birth, a slow torture in the womb,
killing the mother, and the father, fevered
with prophecies, drowns himself
in Holland Bay River.

2/ The Dance Circle

These are virgins in the clearing,
the impromptu jolts of bodies speak
of inexperience, but willingness for the Old.

Listen to their voices, the young tilt
breaking into glass-sparkles in the grass,
watch coral-bead heads, like shields and spears,

clashing; watch dust rising from the 'ring-o'-rosy'
in the alphabet of shells and pea-pods; listen,
their laughter, opening like buds.

The blackest of the virgins, the dark gem
unfurled from a womb long dead,
gazes sad through the darkness.

3/ *Flight*

All me life there were mongrels and cane fields,
blasted idiot people who only abuse me body.
All me life avoided mirrors, me yam nose,
me egg eyes, me monstrosity, me blackness.

All me life Duckenfield made me the celebrated witch.

One before-morning-night, stars outing out,
I take flight through thick bushes, over sharp stones,
bruising me flesh, climbing hills and valleys.

All the while me hear demons behind me,
me hear virulent hisses in the bush,
me feel scraggy hands groping me everywhere.

Across a deep gully, me slip warm and cold
in its belly, it smell green like lime crushed
in mortar, like fever grass boiled too long.
Is there me laugh and dream for a new day.

4/ Sunlight

Sunlight,
leaking from a slash wound
in yellow streams
of brightness.

Sunlight girl
in her summer dress
bouncing.
Watch them boys watching,

sunlight laughing,
how her body moves
without darkness,
without past, in golden
swings and swirls,
a child unhinged to dance.

WOODCUTTER

In the morning, the cedar mind
split open to a bare room
and the fat wife by the coal stove.
Is evil how coal burn from black
to red and the pot of water
hissing like the wife, hissing that she
want more wood axe and how I is man
sleeping till sun hot on God land.
I step off the bed, closer to the heat
of the stove and her body, all the fire,
all the evil heat in the woman
skin and she hissing me,
hissing me outside axing like a jack-
ass, not morning good yet, but fowls
off roost fussing round me
as if I not swinging an axe – should
take one of them head off –
and they scratching between splinters,
and I axing the damn wood, for it is
not morning yet, but Pansy, that fast
neighbour, pissing at her house-side, bawling
her damn lazy boy to get up, how he
want be in bed till God sun on the land.
The axe ring on the wood till sweat
down me back, making stream in me ass.
Last night in the heat of the room,
the woman big hand cross me chest, I
was dreaming a sweat-labour dream,
how I is fifty this month, still going
off to bush, still loading donkey
grass and coming home to the same
woman, and as big as I big,
I can't stop for the little rum, is so
I dream; I labouring and I want

some rum, just a little joy and sweetness.
In the dream I stop at Chung Bar,
that Chiney bitch who if I owe
for a piece of salt-fish, he sending
that damn red gal here, so I stop at Chung
and all of them boys there: I see Alston
and Boy-Boy and Blacka and Courtney and Percival,
all throwing back whites with they face
shine and happy, and as I knock back one,
is the woman that, all the way in me dream,
flinging her fire on me, that I left from morning
and I not back when I know I have to axe
more wood for the fire and she shaming me,
shaming me bad bad, till I lef' and just
like it happening now, I axing wood
with fowls at me foot and the sun barely out.

THE WAR MULE'S ACCOUNT

Now, my business is to cart the dead
from both sides of the Scamander River.
No easy task going through the bustle; spearheads
whizzing my ears – but me, Balthus, I deliver.

My allegiance is to the shades, though I favour
braggadocious Aias (see, I was born behind the walls
now burning), and I like that cadaver-maker,
son of Thetis, the only man out there with balls.

But I hate those snooty black horses in armour,
plumed kingly, stamping fetlocks in the war horde –
those belly-up bastards adored like a good rumour
circling the battlefield, half-happy, half-bored

with the attention showered on them, even by the dying:
"Bless, O gods, let winged Pegasus take me home,"
cried one pathetic brute as his soul came flying
off a bronze dagger that halved his helmet and dome.

I hate especially those so-called immortals,
dropping tears over cut-down Patroklos,
tossing long manes, but never lifting a morsel
of his to the funeral pyre. Man, I cuss

under the heft of Achaeans' and Trojans' weight
I take to the heap; I cuss the carrion kites
and cuss the baying mongrels in wait;
I cuss the long ten years of useless fight.

Yet I harness on, unnoticeable through ranks,
last witness of the city's defeat by a wooden giant,
watching long boats set off on the defiant
Aegean, with loot and women, for distant
islands, not one ever saying "Thanks."

A SURVEYOR'S JOURNAL

for Wilson Harris

I took my name from the aftersky
of a Mesopotamian flood,
birdless as if culture had shed its wings
into a ground vulture on the plain.
Beneath the astral plane, a war-ripped sail,
rigged to its mast, a lantern and a girl,
who swayed and stared
off where the waves raced backwards.
I begged her in signs. She jumped
overboard, arms sieving seaweed, eyes netting home.

Dear Ivy, you live in my veins.
Spurned flesh, I couldn't bridle
the weathervane's shift; it turned and turned
into a landfall, and I, panting panther,
sleek carnivore of the horse-powered limbs,
ran from a reign of terror.
All my despairs in green rain, on leaves;
I prayed to the mantis, head wrapped
in white, reading the "Song of God"
over a bowl of beef. Afterwards,
I hemmed into my skin this hymn:

O lemming souls of the mass migration that ended in drowning
O embroidered heart and marigold wrists that brushed the copper-brown field
O cargoes that left the dengue jungles and ended on the yellow fever shores
O compass points that needled the new to the old, stitching meridians
            into one tense
O reflecting telescope that spied the endangered specimens

Clashing head-brass,
the vertical man vs the horizontal man,

those who lost their surnames
to the sea's ledger, beached up on the strange coast,
waiting for the Star Liner
to cross that imagined Mesopotamian water,
the ship's bulwarks in sleep,
weighed down a spirit-bird,
my calm, to never flounder,
to walk holy and light on this land.

ABENG

The colonel's face turns to mist,
the tasselled-horn trembles in his hand

before he raises it to his lips
and hears a goat's faint wail –

thin like straw grass he blew as a child
at the foot of the Blue Mountain.

They will come soon, the old people,
to the village centre, with no memories,

mist in their eyes, their mouths parched
at the once-a-month ceremonial meeting.

This is how culture dies, the colonel sighs,
watching as smoke goes through the leaves,

joining the horn's call, all one echo;
nothing from Cudjoe, or Queen Nanny,

neither long-head Accompong;
the smoke is just smoke,

but a flight of blackbirds
burst from the treetops.

He lowers the ranking ram's horn,
and says, *At least some still runaway*.

NIGHT FIELD PLEDGE

Strange crafts in the manchineel,
where phantom-men went in and out
of leaves to the stars of Urania,
and remained until morning dew
hardened into a ring encircling
the shattered field. The great hurricane
blanked their minds, poured senses
into Delphi and Atlantis; the birds
took Hades's court of concrete;
they twittered, *to Crete,* in a bull's bust,
its horn-crown formidable as hyphenated
marble. Out of that wrack of logic
came bees, returning the men to light
of brass-gold. They carved an inscription
with their axes for the new world to follow:

      Extinguish Hubris Not Fire.

But someone broke the covenant.
The trees rung with flame for coal.

I who have witnessed will now instruct:

Go out of your gate's gargoyle yawn,
your head shaved and uncovered,
listen for the owl silvered at the neck,
the passing monk dog who knows
the scent of night and the high-pitched
silence of fear – follow him. At the hill's
foot, pledge: *dirt, god, head.*
The dog's tail is white, it ascends
and your spirit leaves. But follow.
At the peak, lamp windows in the woods,
repeat: *dirt, god, head;* fall on your back,

part your lips, for the thousands of bees.
You will be ruptured, but don't cry,
for the night ends at the autumn field
furrowed with stars, your native elements.

NIGHT HAWK

We drummed the stars into nations
of goat skin, hallowed oaks;
the cowbells struck a procession
around the seaside's ring.
When the heave steadied,
a drop-thunder voice parted
our singing – Night Hawk's,
his staff raised, locks shaking,
ember-flitted head, red-eyed chants.
We stay riveted to his bellow;
every torn old testament,
every horned Ge'ez and cave liturgy,
all his stone hymns, falling, until
nothing, nothing but his spread hands,
two wide arcs of winged-cloth.
The sea, and everything below,
listened; all the half-arrived
of the triangular trade,
dead Maroons gathered in trees
along the ridge, woken
by the drowned gong.
A colonel lifted his abeng
and put out the moon.
It could have lasted forever,
but a jeep load of Babylon,
red striped redcoats carrying the veins
of old laws, prowled around him.
He could have been Daniel, Night Hawk,
Shadrach, Meschach and Abednego,
or the fourth man in the furnace,
back straightened up, not of this earth.
Nothing but salt and wind
as we loaded our instruments
in the truck, potholes rehearsing

the bagged shac shac, his phrases
caught in the gearshift, kept changing
as we stared at the moving bush.

RED X

When I was about
    seven years old,
the devil tried to blind
    me with barbwires.

My mother called
    from the yard. Running,
I clashed with the wire –
    I wiped blood from my eyes.

That was the first
    pit the devil dug
before my feet,
    so I would not see
the ill, the corruption,
    the filth, the lies,
the hypocrisy,
    and the order of the day.

THE ENIGMA OF RETURN

Tosh's ghost razors through
Hannah Town, Trench Town,
Tivoli Garden, Waterhouse,
where he had sown a lock
in their dreaded earth.
He sees the same fences, corners,
same natty bald heads talking
the same talk where he last walked,
back with Gong, prophesying
truth in a blood wail old as
the hills and gullies locked in
shingles of sunlight this day of his rise.
The hills have seen eras change,
the gullies felt centuries turned
with a beaten body hiding from
the hound dogs that sniffed his chained feet.
Now, blue uniforms with AK 47s rattle
night leaves where that same body rests.

After masters, after Joshua,
after black prime ministers,
after peace treaty, Coronation Market
still packed like an auction yard,
teeming with crocus-bagged women,
cart boys uprooted from Cockpit
bush side to sweat under
the statue eyes of Queen Victoria;
under her glare Tosh stares at the crab-
in-barrel exchange, the mongrel barter
over ground produce and everything foreign,
until sellers and buyers blur
into a coal heap of transplanted bodies.
This is how black burns out,
how the glow becomes ash,

and, like everything in this rutted road,
overflows to the harbour,
crossing the ancestral ocean.

Yet it is only Saturday market,
for later, under the cover of darkness,
a rum jubilee will break its seal,
and a jamboree of black flesh
will flood speaker-boxed lanes,
coursing on disembodied sounds,
dancing in a ratchet switch of limbs
beneath the blade of the moon.
Tosh knows he must allow them
this happiness, the freedom in dance,
the freedom a man feels when he falls
on his lover's breast at the end of the night.
But that is not now, now they pass
him laughing, *When you laugh I am
condemned, and I see you laugh everyday
and die everyday*, a voice in his head says.
They pass him by, invisible by the Queen,
rigid as holy staff in the afternoon's blaze.

CIRCLE MARCH

The heat cures nothing,
but breeds in every wincing
eye braving the road a frenzy.
I enter the illusion; white
heat levitates my body,
burns my dread roots, settles
and lays all day in my head.
Hysteria quickens bright
slogans on the walls:
green and orange, prisms
of the same blood, coagulated
into one maggot coral.

Congestion thickens;
I vomit back the stale
vision, the bad rum,
the fishbone promises,
the malnourished ear
that sucked the slimiest lie.
The body is a bazaar
of scarce goods on this
campaign's carousel,
drained heads holding
fast to the lizard's tail
that flies the x banner.
I watch the cracked heels
(and I am the cracked heels)
through the hot dust,
marching to the blare
of an ermine, sly gold ring
mouth leader, straight
into Emancipation Park.

THE MIRROR BEFORE SLEEP

The metal-rim mouth garbled
the enamel-spirit I spat out —
my old, man-child desire

to speak without grammar,
to raise the living from the districts' cemetery.
For once I spoke the parable of stones

and words fell from the sky
like burnt leaves chased by boys,
their heads turned into dark clouds.

My voice blazed the cane field,
rows filed into girls' heads and thighs
reaped before their season;

the sun extinguished the square,
brought drought into the old man's throat,
croaking from his piss-parchment rags,

"They wasted me every crop."
Tonight, his withered eyes, the whitewashed plaza,
pack in the mirror before sleep

with the wasted hills and ash barracks,
the stagnant gullies' retching dialect,
the dirt tracks' tongues creasing

into the nightshift ledger, littered with litanies
of shanties in parish St Thomas, with names teeming
to be pronounced. But when my rinsed

mouth opens, nothing; not the moth-fall
of Golden Grove, or the wide sunset-fan
of Peacock Hill, spreading like palm fronds

far from Tropicana's scorched estate.
I may tell all my bones: they look and stare upon me.
Paranoia of the drums and machete —

I am to die, to speak.

THE LAST CIRCLE

When the moon ownself leaps back
globed and dumb into the lime tree,
a goat-head child in a seraph frock

under my window, the sea in my head,
the vision's concentric
ache summons the undead

out of water without panic;
the child avatar gives warning,
names all the districts

death shall visit by morning,
starting with Barracks, then Duckenfield;
the scythe will harvest heads

more than the sea of cane fields;
every hill shall hear the horn
and drop under the sun's wheel;

there first the ants will darn
eyes shut so flies can minister;
worms will have what is scorned;

soldier crabs will fork their dinner
as ombudsmen john crows watch,
peeled-back heads twitching sinister

in tamarind trees, ears cocked to catch
the frequent fall of carcasses,
until the ground is covered in a swatch

of skins and faces vacant as masks,
sinewed tongues knotted in shouts,
spread across shortcuts and passes;

then the dogs will gnaw their mouths,
then the maggots will saw their eyes,
then the beetles will raise their clouts,

then their shades, water-spies,
will be called by the seabirds
to the crossing, two obols for eyes,

gone, not *into the world of light*, but shards
shining into the deep first passage;
a slave sibyl will unbind her chords

and strike a welcome song to assuage
the used-up limbs, skulls white
with horror, eyes-holes daubed

thick with the ever-frightened
look-back for the sliver glint of cane,
the salt hills in the whip-lashed

breeze, paper clouds with ink-stain
seals, the harbours chained in smoke
holding up an exhausted factory name –

Albion Sugar Estate, sending its note
to indentured Indians in soot saris,
to make sacrifice, kill a child and a goat.

NOTES

p. 9. "The Turning Road"
See Andre Derain's painting, *The Turning Road, L'Estaque.*

p. 13. "House on the Hill"
Trakl is the Austrian poet, Georg Trakl (1887-1914).

p. 17. "Catch Fire"
The Babylonian goddess, Ishtar, spoke the line, "I will break the door, wrench the lock, and let in the dead," to the gatekeeper of hell on her descent. Shiduri (sometimes Siduri) is from *Gilgamesh*; she's often compared to Circe of Homer's *Odyssey*.

p. 21. "New World Frescoes"
The epigraph in section VI is from George Seferis's long poem, "Mythistorema", as translated by Edmund Keeley and Philip Sherrard in *Collected Poems*, Princeton University Press, New Jersey, 1995.

p. 27. "A Small Pantheon"
Piscis Austrinus means the "southern fish," one of the forty-eight constellations identified by Ptolemy.

p. 29. "Far District"
"There is nothing here, no visible history, " is a truncated version of James Anthony Froude's (1818-1894) famous, Eurocentric decree about the West Indies, that there is "no people there in the true sense of the word, with a character and purpose of their own." This is from *The English in the West Indies, or The Bow of Ulysses,* Negro Universities Press (reprint), New York, 1969.

p. 46. "Bam-Bam"
The epigraph is from Genesis 6:14.

p. 48. "Walking With Atlas"
Atlas is referring to the Atlas of mythology, but also a security

company in Jamaica of the same name. "Gaulins" is Jamaican patois for egrets, or any bird of that kind.

p. 51. "The Bauble World"
The line: "and he lives by driving his beasts under the sun" is a free translation of the Latin line *flemni feros agitante suos sub sole iugales* by the Jamaican poet and mathematician, Francis Williams (1702-1770). Williams was the first black man enrolled at Cambridge University.

Oriens ex occidente lux – "a light rising from the west" – is the motto of the University of the West Indies. The phrase comes from the English astronomer Jeremiah Horrocks (1618-1641), who predicted and observed the transit of Venus in 1639.

p. 58. "Autobiography of Snow"
"You take off, Harlem or Russia…" between 1922 and 1923, Claude McKay travelled in Russia, where he addressed the Third Communist International in Moscow. See McKay's essay, "Soviet Russia and the Negro".

"O Flame-heart" refers to McKay's poem "Flame-Heart", written in winter. The speaker laments his homesickness for the poinsettia tree of home, "red in warm December".

p. 63. "April"
"*So, waiting, I have won from you the end*" is not Martin Buber's, but from Goethe. The full line is: "So, waiting, I have won from you the end: God's presence in each element."

p. 83. "Red X"
Direct transcription, with some minor tweak, of Peter Tosh's tape-recordings, a kind of audio diary he made prior to his death in 1987. See the 1992 documentary *Stepping Razor: Red X.*

p. 87. "The Mirror Before Sleep"
Italicized line is from Psalm 22:17.

p. 89. "The Last Circle"
Into the world of light refers to Henry Vaughn's poem that begins "They are all gone into the world of light!"

ABOUT THE AUTHOR

Ishion Hutchinson was born in Port Antonio, Jamaica. He attended the University of the West Indies, Mona, and received his MFA in Poetry from New York University. A recipient of a Derek Walcott Fellowship, a Calabash Literary Fellowship, and a Cropper Foundation Fellowship, Ishion Hutchinson is a founding member of *The Workshop*, a UWI-based collective that held writing workshops on the Mona Campus. He has taught Creative Writing at NYU and tutored high school students at the Steinhardt School of Culture, Education, and Human Development. He has presented his work at the Emerging Writers Series at NYU, the Brandeis University Festival of the Creative Arts, and the Working Dog Reading Series at the University of Utah, where he holds a Vice-Presidential Scholarship and is completing his PhD in English and Creative Writing. His poetry and essays have appeared in such publications as *Attica Journal, Callaloo Journal, Caribbean Review of Books, Expressions, The LA Review, The Jamaica Sunday Gleaner,* and *Pathway.* In 2006, the Calabash Trust Fund published his chapbook, *Bryan's Bay*. *Far District* is his first book.

NEW AND RECENT POETRY FROM PEEPAL TREE

Christian Campbell
Running the Dusk
ISBN: 9781845231552; pp. 84, April 2010; £8.99

Christian Campbell takes us to dusk, what the French call *l'heure entre chien et loup*, the hour between dog and wolf, to explore ambiguity and intersection, danger and desire, loss and possibility. These poems of wild imagination shift shape and shift generation, remapping Caribbean, British and African American geographies: Oxford becomes Oxfraud; Shabba Ranks duets with Césaire; Sidney Poitier is reconsidered in an exam question; market women hawk poetry beside knock-off Gucci bags; elegies for ancestors are also for land and sea. Here is dancing at the crossroads between reverence and irreverence. Dusk is memory, dusk is dream, dusk is a way to re-imagine the past.

Kwame Dawes
Back of Mount Peace
ISBN: 9781845231248; pp. 96, December 2009; £8.99

A retired fisherman, Monty Cupidon, encounters a naked, bloodied and traumatised woman standing at the cross-roads. He offers comfort and takes her in. Suffering from amnesia, she cannot tell him anything about herself. The only clues are the signs that she has once worn a wedding ring, has a butterfly tattoo and red nail polish on her toes. In the absence of memory, he names her Esther. So begins a remarkable sequence of poems that explores many dimensions of liminality. *Back of Mount Peace* explores the space between body and mind, making Esther's halting discovery of her self through her body, which like a tree bears its indelible history, work both as moving narrative device and a deeply sensual reminder of the physicality of existence.

Above all, this is a sequence that explores a relationship which begins in a primal Edenic space of innocent discovery in which, as Monty hopes, 'the hallelujah's of new love will begin', but which, like all relationships must enter history, the decay of time and the corruptions of knowledge..

Jacqueline Bishop
Snapshots from Istanbul
ISBN: 9781845231149; pp. 80, April 2009; £7.99

Framed by poems that explore the lives of the exiled Roman poet
Ovid, and the journeying painter Gaugin, Bishop, already between
Jamaica and the USA, locates her own explorations of where home
might be. This is tested in a sequence of sensuous poems about a
doomed relationship in Istanbul, touching in its honesty and, though
vivid in its portrayal of otherness, highly aware that the poems' true
subject is the uprooted self.

Millicent A.A. Graham
The Damp in Things
ISBN: 9781845230838; pp. 56, May 2009; £7.99

In *The Damp in Things*, we are invited into the unique imagination of
Millicent Graham: she offers us a way to see her distinctly contem-
porary and urban Jamaica through the slant eye of a surrealist, one
willing to see the absurdities and contradictions inherent in its
society. These are poems about family, love, spirituality, fear, and
above all desire, where the dampness of things is as much about the
humid sensuality of this woman's island as it is about her constant
belief in fecundity, fertility and the unruliness of the imagination.
deeply aware of the value of both homage and resistance. The result is
a wonderfully executed balancing act that ultimately suggests a newness
of sensibility and imagination.

All Peepal Tree titles are available from the website
www.peepaltreepress.com
with a money back guarantee, secure credit card ordering
and fast delivery throughout the world at cost or less.

Contact us at:
Peepal Tree Press, 17 King's Avenue, Leeds LS6 1QS, UK
Tel: +44 (0) 113 2451703 E-mail: contact@peepaltreepress.com